Classroom Rules

Betsy Franco
Photographs by Ken O'Donoghue

We have classroom rules.
Rules help us and
keep us safe.

Classroom Rules

Rule 1: Share.

Rule 2: Be a helper.

Rule 3: Talk about it.

Rule 4: Put up your hand to talk.

Rule 5: Take turns.

Rule 1: Share.

We all want to use
the new box of crayons.
We know what to do.
We can share the crayons!

Classroom Rules

Rule 1: Share.

Rule 2: Be a helper.

Rule 3: Talk about it.

Rule 4: Put up your hand to ta

Rule 5: Take turns.

I Looked Through My Window

Michaela Morgan
Illustrated by Anthony Lewis

Rule 2: Be a helper.

Our teacher needs
to pass out papers.
There are so many papers!
We can pass out the papers
to help the teacher.

Classroom Rules

Rule 1: Share.

Rule 2: Be a helper.

Rule 3: Talk about it.

Rule 4: Put up your hand to talk.

Rule 5: Take turns.

I Looked Through My **Window**

Rule 3: Talk about it.

Jill broke Rafi's pencil.
Rafi is mad.

Classroom Rules

Rule 1: Share.

Rule 2: Be a helper.

Rule 3: Talk about it.

Rule 4: Put up your hand to talk.

Rule 5: Take turns.

9

Jill and Rafi don't hit and shout.
They talk about it.
Jill gives Rafi one of her pencils.

Rule 4: Put up your hand to talk.

Carmen wants to say something.
What should she do?
She puts up her hand.
Then the teacher will let her talk.

Classroom Rules

Rule 1: Share.

Rule 2: Be a helper.

Rule 3: Talk about it.

Rule 4: Put up your hand to talk.

Rule 5: Take turns.

On Monday morning,
Molly Mack
went to the market
with a sunshade and a sack,
went to the market
with a sunshade and a sack,
and a parrot on her shoulder
called Kakadu Jack.

Kakadu Jack
Kakadu Jack
A parrot on her shoulder
called Kakadu Jack.

I Looked Through
My **Window**

Michaela Morgan
Illustrated by Anthony Lewis

13

Rule 5: Take turns.

We are playing
with the class pet.
Everyone wants to give him food.
We don't grab or push.
We take turns and
have more fun that way.

Classroom Rules

Rule 1: Share.

Rule 2: Be a helper.

Rule 3: Talk about it.

Rule 4: Put up your hand to talk.

Rule 5: Take turns.

I Looked Through My **Window**

15

Now you know
our classroom rules.
Rules help us,
and rules keep us safe!

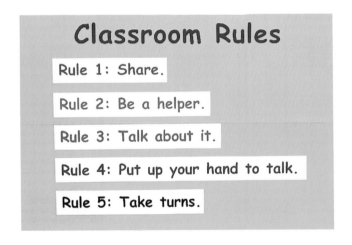

Classroom Rules

Rule 1: Share.

Rule 2: Be a helper.

Rule 3: Talk about it.

Rule 4: Put up your hand to talk.

Rule 5: Take turns.